WORDS OF HOPE™

AMAZING GRACE

D1742587

christian
art gifts®

Amazing Grace

© 2016 Christian Art Gifts, RSA
        Christian Art Gifts Inc., IL, USA

First edition 2016

Designed by Christian Art Gifts

Images used under license from Shutterstock.com

Printed in China

ISBN 978-1-4321-1616-3

AMAZING GRACE

Amazing grace! How sweet the sound
that saved a wretch like me!
I once was lost, but now am found;
was blind, but now I see.
'Twas grace that taught my heart to fear,
and grace my fears relieved;
how precious did that grace appear
the hour I first believed.
Through many dangers, toils and snares,
I have already come;
'tis grace hath brought me safe thus far,
and grace will lead me home.
The Lord has promised good to me,
His Word my hope secures;
He will my Shield and Portion be,
as long as life endures.
Yea, when this flesh and heart shall fail,
and mortal life shall cease,
I shall possess, within the veil,
a life of joy and peace.
The earth shall soon dissolve like snow,
the sun forbear to shine;
but God, who called me here below,
will be forever mine.
When we've been there ten thousand years,
bright shining as the sun,
we've no less days to sing God's praise
than when we'd first begun.

John Newton (1725 - 1807)

Contents

Amazing Grace! How sweet the sound ...

God's Amazing Grace 10

The Sweet Sound of Salvation 17

'Twas grace that taught my heart to fear ...

Reverence for the Lord 25

Fears Relieved 32

Strong Faith 39

Through many dangers, toils and snares ...

Times of Tribulation 47

God Leads Us Safely Home 54

The Lord has promised good to me ...

Assurance of Blessings 62

The Word of God 69

God Is Our Shield and Portion 76

Yea, when this flesh and heart shall fail ...

A Life of Joy...84

Finding Peace..91

The earth shall soon dissolve like snow ...

Called by God 99

Eternal Life with the Lord 106

When we've been there ten thousand years ...

Praise the Lord...114

Thank the Lord...121

Amazing Grace!

How sweet the sound
that *saved* a wretch like me!
I once was lost,
but now am *found;*
was blind,
but now I see.

GOD'S AMAZING GRACE

To each one of us grace has been given as Christ apportioned it. This is why it says: "When He ascended on high, He took many captives and gave gifts to His people."

Ephesians 4:7-8 NIV

He said to me, "My grace is sufficient for you, for My power is made perfect in weakness." Therefore I will boast all the more gladly of my weaknesses, so that the power of Christ may rest upon me. For the sake of Christ, then, I am content with weaknesses, insults, hardships, persecutions, and calamities. For when I am weak, then I am strong.

2 Corinthians 12:9-10 ESV

GOD'S AMAZING GRACE

God can point to us in all future ages as examples of the incredible wealth of His grace and kindness toward us, as shown in all He has done for us who are united with Christ Jesus. God saved you by His grace when you believed. And you can't take credit for this; it is a gift from God.

Ephesians 2:7-8 NLT

God is able to make all grace abound to you, so that having all sufficiency in all things at all times, you may abound in every good work.

2 Corinthians 9:8 ESV

Sin is no longer your master, for you no longer live under the requirements of the law. Instead, you live under the freedom of God's grace.

Romans 6:14 NLT

 # GOD'S AMAZING GRACE

For the grace of God has appeared, bringing salvation for all people.

Titus 2:11 ESV

From His abundance we have all received one gracious blessing after another.

John 1:16 NLT

The LORD is compassionate and gracious, slow to anger, abounding in love. He does not treat us as our sins deserve or repay us according to our iniquities. For as high as the heavens are above the earth, so great is His love for those who fear Him; as far as the east is from the west, so far has He removed our transgressions from us.

Psalm 103:8, 10-12 NIV

GOD'S AMAZING GRACE

Through Him we have also obtained access by faith into this grace in which we stand, and we rejoice in hope of the glory of God.

Romans 5:2 ESV

We are all saved the same way, by the undeserved grace of the Lord Jesus.

Acts 15:11 NLT

I commend you to God and to the word of His grace, which is able to build you up and to give you the inheritance among all those who are sanctified.

Acts 20:32 ESV

GOD'S AMAZING GRACE

You know the generous grace of our Lord Jesus Christ. Though He was rich, yet for your sakes He became poor, so that by His poverty He could make you rich.

2 Corinthians 8:9 NLT

May our Lord Jesus Christ Himself and God our Father, who loved us and by His grace gave us eternal encouragement and good hope, encourage your hearts and strengthen you in every good deed and word.

2 Thessalonians 2:16-17 NIV

We praise God for the glorious grace He has poured out on us who belong to His dear Son.

Ephesians 1:6 NLT

GOD'S AMAZING GRACE

May you experience the love of Christ, though it is too great to understand fully. Then you will be made complete with all the fullness of life and power that comes from God.

Ephesians 3:19 NLT

The God of all grace, who called you to His eternal glory in Christ, after you have suffered a little while, will Himself restore you and make you strong, firm and steadfast.

1 Peter 5:10 NIV

Even before I was born, God chose me and called me by His marvelous grace.

Galatians 1:15 NLT

The LORD will give grace and glory; no good thing will He withhold from those who walk uprightly.

Psalm 84:11 NKJV

Because of His grace He declared us righteous and gave us confidence that we will inherit eternal life.

Titus 3:7 NLT

Let us then approach God's throne of grace with confidence, so that we may receive mercy and find grace to help us in our time of need.

Hebrews 4:16 NIV

THE SWEET SOUND OF SALVATION

So prepare your minds for action and exercise self-control. Put all your hope in the gracious salvation that will come to you when Jesus Christ is revealed to the world.

1 Peter 1:13 NLT

Sing to the LORD, bless His name; proclaim the good news of His salvation from day to day.

Psalm 96:2 NKJV

If we walk in the light, as He is in the light, we have fellowship with one another, and the blood of Jesus His Son cleanses us from all sin.

1 John 1:7 NIV

"Most assuredly, I say to you, I am the door of the sheep. All who ever came before Me are thieves and robbers, but the sheep did not hear them. I am the door. If anyone enters by Me, he will be saved, and will go in and out and find pasture. The thief does not come except to steal, and to kill, and to destroy. I have come that they may have life, and that they may have it more abundantly."

John 10:7-10 NKJV

Jesus is the stone that was rejected by you, the builders, which has become the cornerstone. And there is salvation in no one else, for there is no other name under heaven given among men by which we must be saved.

Acts 4:11-12 ESV

THE SWEET SOUND OF SALVATION

In Him we have redemption through His blood, the forgiveness of sins, in accordance with the riches of God's grace that He lavished on us.

Ephesians 1:7-8 NIV

The LORD takes pleasure in His people; He will beautify the humble with salvation.

Psalm 149:4 NKJV

Praise be to the Lord, to God our Savior, who daily bears our burdens. Our God is a God who saves; from the Sovereign LORD comes escape from death.

Psalm 68:19-20 NIV

THE SWEET SOUND OF SALVATION

"Those who listen to My message and believe in God who sent Me have eternal life. They will never be condemned for their sins, but they have already passed from death into life."

John 5:24 NLT

"My sheep hear My voice, and I know them, and they follow Me. And I give them eternal life, and they shall never perish; neither shall anyone snatch them out of My hand. My Father, who has given them to Me, is greater than all; and no one is able to snatch them out of My Father's hand."

John 10:27-29 NKJV

I have trusted in Your steadfast love; my heart shall rejoice in Your salvation.

Psalm 13:5 ESV

THE SWEET SOUND OF SALVATION

"All those the Father gives Me will come to Me, and whoever comes to Me I will never drive away. For I have come down from heaven not to do My will but to do the will of Him who sent Me. And this is the will of Him who sent Me, that I shall lose none of all those He has given Me, but raise them up at the last day."

John 6:37-39 NIV

For the Scripture says, "Whoever believes on Him will not be put to shame." For there is no distinction between Jew and Greek, for the same Lord over all is rich to all who call upon Him. For "whoever calls on the name of the LORD shall be saved."

Romans 10:11-13 NKJV

THE SWEET SOUND OF SALVATION

I delight greatly in the LORD; my soul rejoices in my God. For He has clothed me with garments of salvation and arrayed me in a robe of His righteousness.

Isaiah 61:10 NIV

It is good that one should hope and wait quietly for the salvation of the LORD.

Lamentations 3:26 NKJV

He is able to save to the uttermost those who draw near to God through Him, since He always lives to make intercession for them.

Hebrews 7:25 ESV

THE SWEET SOUND OF SALVATION

Believe in the Lord Jesus, and you will be saved, you and your household.

Acts 16:31 ESV

If you openly declare that Jesus is Lord and believe in your heart that God raised Him from the dead, you will be saved. For it is by believing in your heart that you are made right with God, and it is by openly declaring your faith that you are saved.

Romans 10;9-10 NLT

Restore to me the joy of Your salvation and grant me a willing spirit, to sustain me.

Psalm 51:12 NIV

'Twas grace that taught my *heart* to fear, and grace my fears relieved; how *precious* did that grace appear the hour I first *believed*.

REVERENCE FOR THE LORD

Since we are receiving a Kingdom that is unshakable, let us be thankful and please God by worshiping Him with holy fear and awe. For our God is a devouring fire.

Hebrews 12:28-29 NLT

Be sure to fear the LORD and serve Him faithfully with all your heart; consider what great things He has done for you.

1 Samuel 12:24 NIV

In mercy and truth atonement is provided for iniquity; and by the fear of the LORD one departs from evil.

Proverbs 16:6 NKJV

"I tell you, My friends, do not be afraid of those who kill the body and after that can do no more. But I will show you whom you should fear: Fear Him who, after your body has been killed, has authority to throw you into hell. Yes, I tell you, fear Him."

Luke 12:4-5 NIV

From the throne came a voice saying, "Praise our God, all you His servants, you who fear Him, small and great."

Revelation 19:5 ESV

Honor all people. Love the brotherhood. Fear God.

1 Peter 2:17 NKJV

REVERENCE FOR THE LORD

"Do not curse the deaf or put a stumbling block in front of the blind, but fear your God. I am the LORD."

Leviticus 19:14 NIV

How joyful are those who fear the LORD – all who follow His ways! You will enjoy the fruit of your labor. How joyful and prosperous you will be!

Psalm 128:1-2 NLT

Reverence for the LORD is pure, lasting forever. The laws of the LORD are true; each one is fair. They are more desirable than gold, even the finest gold.

Psalm 19:9-10 NLT

REVERENCE FOR THE LORD

The fear of the LORD is the beginning of wisdom; a good understanding have all those who do His commandments. His praise endures forever.

Psalm 111:10 NKJV

His delight is not in the strength of the horse, nor His pleasure in the legs of a man, but the LORD takes pleasure in those who fear Him, in those who hope in His steadfast love.

Psalm 147:10-11 ESV

The angel of the LORD encamps all around those who fear Him, and delivers them.

Psalm 34:7 NKJV

REVERENCE FOR THE LORD

Whoever fears the LORD has a secure fortress, and for their children it will be a refuge. The fear of the LORD is a fountain of life, turning a person from the snares of death.

Proverbs 14:26-27 NIV

Fear God and keep His commandments, for this is the whole duty of man.

Ecclesiastes 12:13 ESV

Let the whole world fear the LORD, and let everyone stand in awe of Him. For when He spoke, the world began! It appeared at His command.

Psalm 33:8-9 NLT

REVERENCE FOR THE LORD

The Mighty One has done great things for me –
holy is His name. His mercy extends to those
who fear Him, from generation to generation.

Luke 1:49-50 NIV

Fear the LORD, you His godly people, for those
who fear Him will have all they need.

Psalm 34:9 NLT

Do not be wise in your own eyes; fear the LORD
and depart from evil. It will be health to your
flesh, and strength to your bones.

Proverbs 3:7-8 NKJV

REVERENCE FOR THE LORD

Let us purify ourselves from everything that contaminates body and spirit, perfecting holiness out of reverence for God.

2 Corinthians 7:1 NIV

Serve only the LORD your God and fear Him alone. Obey His commands, listen to His voice, and cling to Him.

Deuteronomy 13:4 NLT

"Do not be afraid of those who kill the body but cannot kill the soul. Rather, be afraid of the One who can destroy both soul and body in hell."

Matthew 10:28 NIV

FEARS RELIEVED

He will cover you with His pinions, and under His wings you will find refuge; His faithfulness is a shield and buckler. You will not fear the terror of the night, nor the arrow that flies by day, nor the pestilence that stalks in darkness, nor the destruction that wastes at noonday.

Psalm 91:4-6 ESV

"So do not fear, for I am with you; do not be dismayed, for I am your God."

Isaiah 41:10 NIV

The LORD is my light and my salvation; whom shall I fear? The LORD is the strength of my life; of whom shall I be afraid?

Psalm 27:1 NKJV

Even though I walk through the valley of the shadow of death, I will fear no evil, for You are with me; Your rod and Your staff, they comfort me.

Psalm 23:4 ESV

Be strong, and do not fear, for your God is coming to destroy your enemies. He is coming to save you.

Isaiah 35:4 NLT

"I am the LORD your God who takes hold of your right hand and says to you, Do not fear; I will help you."

Isaiah 41:13 NIV

FEARS RELIEVED

Be strong and courageous. Do not be afraid
or terrified because of them, for the LORD
your God goes with you; He will never leave
you nor forsake you.

Deuteronomy 31:6 NIV

Have I not commanded you? Be strong and
courageous. Do not be frightened, and do not
be dismayed, for the LORD your God is with you
wherever you go.

Joshua 1:9 ESV

"Fear not, little flock, for it is your Father's
good pleasure to give you the kingdom."

Luke 12:32 ESV

God is our refuge and strength, an ever-present help in trouble. Therefore we will not fear, though the earth give way and the mountains fall into the heart of the sea.

Psalm 46:1-2 NIV

We can say with confidence, "The LORD is my helper, so I will have no fear. What can mere people do to me?"

Hebrews 13:6 NLT

The fear of man brings a snare, but whoever trusts in the LORD shall be safe.

Proverbs 29:25 NKJV

FEARS RELIEVED

God has not given us a spirit of fear and timidity, but of power, love, and self-discipline.

2 Timothy 1:7 NLT

Oh, magnify the LORD with me, and let us exalt His name together! I sought the LORD, and He answered me and delivered me from all my fears.

Psalm 34:3-4 ESV

There is no fear in love. But perfect love drives out fear, because fear has to do with punishment. The one who fears is not made perfect in love.

1 John 4:18 NIV

FEARS RELIEVED

When I am afraid, I will put my trust in You.

Psalm 56:3 NLT

"Are not two sparrows sold for a copper coin? And not one of them falls to the ground apart from your Father's will. But the very hairs of your head are all numbered. Do not fear therefore; you are of more value than many sparrows."

Matthew 10:29-31 NKJV

Out of my distress I called on the LORD; the LORD answered me and set me free. The LORD is on my side; I will not fear. What can man do to me? The LORD is on my side as my helper; I shall look in triumph on those who hate me.

Psalm 118:5-7 ESV

FEARS RELIEVED

In God I have put my trust; I will not fear. What can flesh do to me?

Psalm 56:4 NKJV

Cast all your anxiety on Him because He cares for you.

1 Peter 5:7 NIV

All who are led by the Spirit of God are children of God. So you have not received a spirit that makes you fearful slaves. Instead, you received God's Spirit when He adopted you as His own children. Now we call Him, "Abba, Father."

Romans 8:14-15 NLT

Jesus said, "All things are possible for one who believes."

Mark 9:23 ESV

Then Jesus told them, "I tell you the truth, if you have faith and don't doubt, you can do things like this and much more. You can even say to this mountain, 'May you be lifted up and thrown into the sea,' and it will happen."

Matthew 21:21 NLT

We fix our eyes not on what is seen, but on what is unseen, since what is seen is temporary, but what is unseen is eternal.

2 Corinthians 4:18 NIV

"If you had faith even as small as a mustard seed, you could say to this mountain, 'Move from here to there,' and it would move. Nothing would be impossible."

Matthew 17:20 NLT

Be on your guard; stand firm in the faith; be courageous; be strong.

1 Corinthians 16:13 NIV

Now faith is the substance of things hoped for, the evidence of things not seen.

Hebrews 11:1 NKJV

We live by faith, not by sight.

2 Corinthians 5:7 NIV

STRONG FAITH

I am not ashamed of the gospel, because it is the power of God that brings salvation to everyone who believes. For in the gospel the righteousness of God is revealed – a righteousness that is by faith from first to last, just as it is written: "The righteous will live by faith."

Romans 1:16-17 NIV

Because of Christ and our faith in Him, we can now come boldly and confidently into God's presence.

Ephesians 3:12 NLT

In all circumstances take up the shield of faith, with which you can extinguish all the flaming darts of the evil one.

Ephesians 6:16 ESV

STRONG FAITH

Trust in the LORD with all your heart; do not depend on your own understanding. Seek His will in all you do, and He will show you which path to take.

Proverbs 3:5-6 NLT

What good is it if someone claims to have faith but has no deeds? Can such faith save them? Suppose a brother or a sister is without clothes and daily food. If one of you says to them, "Go in peace; keep warm and well fed," but does nothing about their physical needs, what good is it? In the same way, faith by itself, if it is not accompanied by action, is dead. But someone will say, "You have faith; I have deeds." Show me your faith without deeds, and I will show you my faith by my deeds.

James 2:14-18 NIV

STRONG FAITH

Make every effort to supplement your faith with virtue, and virtue with knowledge, and knowledge with self-control, and self-control with steadfastness, and steadfastness with godliness, and godliness with brotherly affection, and brotherly affection with love.

2 Peter 1:5-7 ESV

Be truly glad. There is wonderful joy ahead, even though you must endure many trials for a little while. These trials will show that your faith is genuine. It is being tested as fire tests and purifies gold – though your faith is far more precious than mere gold. So when your faith remains strong through many trials, it will bring you much praise and glory and honor on the day when Jesus Christ is revealed to the whole world.

1 Peter 1:6-7 NLT

Faith comes from hearing the message, and the message is heard through the word about Christ.

Romans 10:17 NIV

Without faith it is impossible to please Him, for he who comes to God must believe that He is, and that He is a rewarder of those who diligently seek Him.

Hebrews 11:6 NKJV

Everyone who believes that Jesus is the Christ has been born of God, and everyone who loves the Father loves whoever has been born of Him.

1 John 5:1 ESV

STRONG FAITH

We know that a person is made right with God by faith in Jesus Christ, not by obeying the law. And we have believed in Christ Jesus, so that we might be made right with God because of our faith in Christ, not because we have obeyed the law. For no one will ever be made right with God by obeying the law.

Galatians 2:16 NLT

If any of you lacks wisdom, let him ask God, who gives generously to all without reproach, and it will be given him. But let him ask in faith, with no doubting, for the one who doubts is like a wave of the sea that is driven and tossed by the wind. For that person must not suppose that he will receive anything from the Lord; he is a double-minded man, unstable in all his ways.

James 1:5-8 ESV

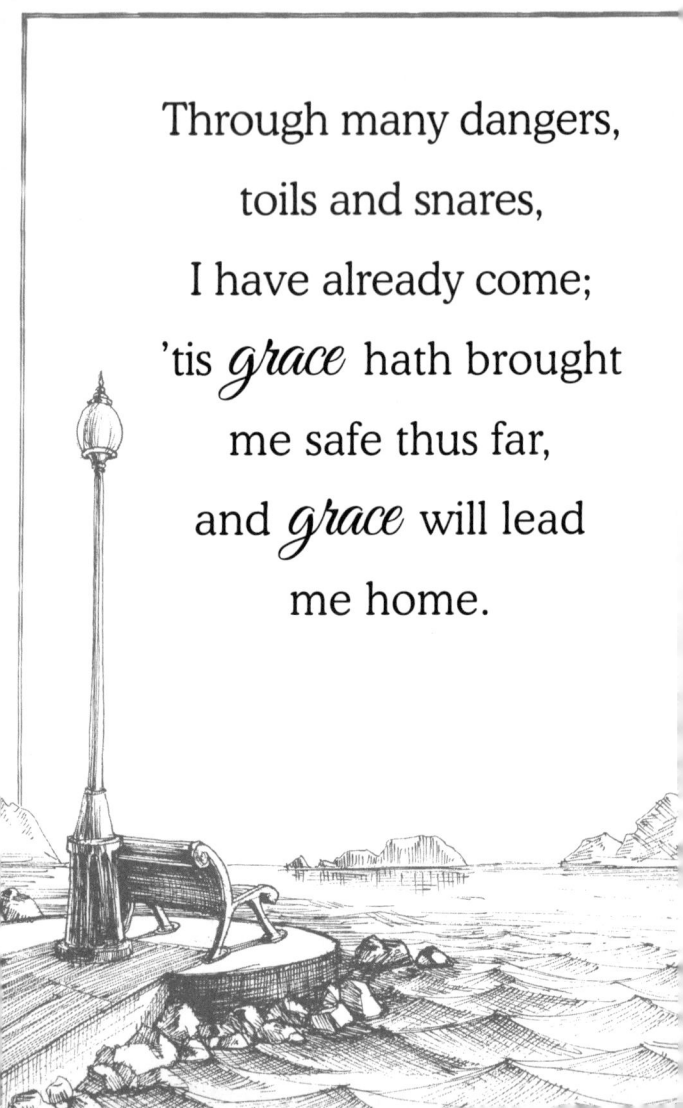

Through many dangers, toils and snares, I have already come; 'tis *grace* hath brought me safe thus far, and *grace* will lead me home.

Blessed is the one who perseveres under trial because, having stood the test, that person will receive the crown of life.

James 1:12 NIV

We rejoice in our sufferings, knowing that suffering produces endurance, and endurance produces character, and character produces hope, and hope does not put us to shame, because God's love has been poured into our hearts through the Holy Spirit who has been given to us.

Romans 5:3-5 ESV

Since He Himself has gone through suffering and testing, He is able to help us when we are being tested.

Hebrews 2:18 NLT

Consider it pure joy, my brothers and sisters, whenever you face trials of many kinds, because you know that the testing of your faith develops perseverance. Let perseverance finish its work so that you may be mature and complete, not lacking anything.

James 1:2-4 NIV

I consider that the sufferings of this present time are not worth comparing with the glory that is to be revealed to us.

Romans 8:18 ESV

The more we suffer for Christ, the more God will shower us with His comfort through Christ.

2 Corinthians 1:5 NLT

TIMES OF TRIBULATION

Beloved, do not think it strange concerning the fiery trial which is to try you, as though some strange thing happened to you; but rejoice to the extent that you partake of Christ's sufferings, that when His glory is revealed, you may also be glad with exceeding joy.

1 Peter 4:12-13 NKJV

God had planned something better for us.

Hebrews 11:40 NIV

As the elect of God, holy and beloved, put on tender mercies, kindness, humility, meekness, longsuffering.

Colossians 3:12 NKJV

Those who suffer according to God's will should commit themselves to their faithful Creator and continue to do good.

1 Peter 4:19 NIV

When you go through deep waters, I will be with you. When you go through rivers of difficulty, you will not drown. When you walk through the fire of oppression, you will not be burned up; the flames will not consume you.

Isaiah 43:2 NLT

I love the Lord because He hears my voice and my prayer for mercy. Because He bends down to listen, I will pray as long as I have breath!

Psalm 116:1-2 NLT

If you suffer for doing good and you endure it, this is commendable before God.

1 Peter 2:20 NIV

Be strong and do not give up, for your work will be rewarded.

2 Chronicles 15:7 NIV

The Lord knows how to rescue godly people from their trials.

2 Peter 2:9 NLT

What we suffer now is nothing compared to the glory He will reveal to us later.

Romans 8:18 NLT

Let us throw off everything that hinders and the sin that so easily entangles. And let us run with perseverance the race marked out for us, fixing our eyes on Jesus, the pioneer and perfecter of faith.

Hebrews 12:1-2 NIV

"Don't let your hearts be troubled. Trust in God, and trust also in Me."

John 14:1 NLT

The Lord sustains them on their sickbed and restores them from their bed of illness.

Psalm 41:3 NIV

The LORD hears His people when they call to Him for help. He rescues them from all their troubles.

Psalm 34:17 NLT

The LORD is a stronghold for the oppressed, a stronghold in times of trouble. And those who know Your name put their trust in You, for You, O LORD, have not forsaken those who seek You.

Psalm 9:9-10 ESV

Share each other's burdens, and in this way obey the law of Christ.

Galatians 6:2 NLT

GOD LEADS US SAFELY HOME

The LORD will guide you always; He will satisfy your needs in a sun-scorched land and will strengthen your frame. You will be like a well-watered garden, like a spring whose waters never fail.

Isaiah 58:11 NIV

Jesus said to him, "I am the way, the truth, and the life. No one comes to the Father except through Me."

John 14:6 NKJV

Show me Your ways, LORD, teach me Your paths. Guide me in Your truth and teach me, for You are God my Savior, and my hope is in You all day long.

Psalm 25:4-5 NIV

GOD LEADS US SAFELY HOME

Send out Your light and Your truth; let them guide me. Let them lead me to Your holy mountain, to the place where You live. There I will go to the altar of God, to God – the source of all my joy.

Psalm 43:3-4 NLT

"Call to Me, and I will answer you, and show you great and mighty things, which you do not know."

Jeremiah 33:3 NKJV

Your word is a lamp to guide my feet and a light for my path.

Psalm 119:105 NLT

GOD LEADS US SAFELY HOME

Teach me to do Your will, for You are my God! Let Your good Spirit lead me on level ground! For Your name's sake, O Lord, preserve my life! In Your righteousness bring my soul out of trouble!

Psalm 143:10-11 ESV

May the Lord direct your hearts into God's love and Christ's perseverance.

2 Thessalonians 3:5 NIV

The Lord directs the steps of the godly. He delights in every detail of their lives. Though they stumble, they will never fall, for the Lord holds them by the hand.

Psalm 37:23-24 NLT

GOD LEADS US SAFELY HOME

Whether you turn to the right or to the left, your ears will hear a voice behind you, saying, "This is the way; walk in it."

Isaiah 30:21 NIV

The LORD is good and does what is right; He shows the proper path to those who go astray.

Psalm 25:8 NLT

The LORD says, "I will guide you along the best pathway for your life. I will advise you and watch over you."

Psalm 32:8 NLT

GOD LEADS US SAFELY HOME

"I will go before you and make the crooked places straight; I will break in pieces the gates of bronze and cut the bars of iron. I will give you the treasures of darkness and hidden riches of secret places, that you may know that I, the LORD, who call you by your name, am the God of Israel."

Isaiah 45:2-3 NKJV

God is our God for ever and ever; He will be our guide even to the end.

Psalm 48:14 NIV

Direct my steps by Your word, and let no iniquity have dominion over me.

Psalm 119:133 NKJV

GOD LEADS US SAFELY HOME

May He give you the desire of your heart and make all your plans succeed.

Psalm 20:4 NIV

Put your hope in the LORD. Travel steadily along His path.

Psalm 37:34 NLT

The word of the LORD is upright, and all His work is done in faithfulness.

Psalm 33:4 ESV

You will show me the way of life, granting me the joy of Your presence and the pleasures of living with You forever.

Psalm 16:11 NLT

GOD LEADS US SAFELY HOME

He leads the humble in doing right, teaching them His way. The LORD leads with unfailing love and faithfulness all who keep His covenant and obey His demands.

Psalm 25:9-10 NLT

A man's heart plans his way, but the LORD directs his steps.

Proverbs 16:9 NKJV

The counsel of the LORD stands forever, the plans of His heart to all generations.

Psalm 33:11 ESV

The Lord has
promised good to me,
His Word my hope secures;
He will my Shield
and Portion be,
as long as life *endures*.

The curse of the LORD is on the house of the wicked, but He blesses the home of the just.

Proverbs 3:33 NKJV

May the LORD cause you to flourish, both you and your children. May you be blessed by the LORD, the Maker of heaven and earth.

Psalm 115:14-15 NIV

When You open Your hand, You satisfy the hunger and thirst of every living thing. The LORD is righteous in everything He does; He is filled with kindness.

Psalm 145:16-17 NLT

"Blessed are those who hunger and thirst for righteousness, for they shall be satisfied."

Matthew 5:6 ESV

Blessed are those who trust in the Lord and have made the Lord their hope and confidence.

Jeremiah 17:7 NLT

Blessed are those whose way is blameless, who walk in the law of the Lord!

Psalm 119:1 ESV

The blessing of the Lord brings wealth, without painful toil for it.

Proverbs 10:22 NIV

"God blesses those who are poor and realize their need for Him, for the Kingdom of Heaven is theirs."

Matthew 5:3 NLT

Oh, taste and see that the LORD is good; blessed is the man who trusts in Him!

Psalm 34:8 NKJV

The LORD will indeed give what is good, and our land will yield its harvest.

Psalm 85:12 NIV

"Blessed are those who mourn, for they shall be comforted."

Matthew 5:4 ESV

"Blessed are the pure in heart, for they shall see God."

Matthew 5:8 NKJV

"Bring all the tithes into the storehouse so there will be enough food in My Temple. If you do," says the LORD of Heaven's Armies, "I will open the windows of heaven for you. I will pour out a blessing so great you won't have enough room to take it in! Try it! Put Me to the test!"

Malachi 3:10 NLT

The LORD will make you abound in prosperity ... The LORD will open to you His good treasury, the heavens, to give the rain to your land in its season and to bless all the work of your hands.

Deuteronomy 28:11-12 ESV

ASSURANCE OF BLESSINGS

The LORD bless you and keep you; the LORD make His face shine upon you, and be gracious to you; the LORD lift up His countenance upon you, and give you peace.

Numbers 6:24-26 NKJV

"God blesses those who are merciful, for they will be shown mercy."

Matthew 5:7 NLT

The LORD is my chosen portion and my cup; You hold my lot. The lines have fallen for me in pleasant places; indeed, I have a beautiful inheritance.

Psalm 16:5-6 ESV

All praise to God, the Father of our Lord Jesus Christ, who has blessed us with every spiritual blessing in the heavenly realms because we are united with Christ.

Ephesians 1:3 NLT

"Blessed are the meek, for they will inherit the earth."

Matthew 5:5 NIV

You go before me and follow me. You place Your hand of blessing on my head. Such knowledge is too wonderful for me, too great for me to understand!

Psalm 139:5-6 NLT

The Lord your God will bless you in all your harvest and in all the work of your hands, and your joy will be complete.

Deuteronomy 16:15 NIV

"I will bless those who have humble and contrite hearts, who tremble at My word."

Isaiah 66:2 NLT

"Blessed are those who are persecuted for righteousness' sake, for theirs is the kingdom of heaven."

Matthew 5:10 NKJV

THE WORD OF GOD

All Scripture is inspired by God and is useful to teach us what is true and to make us realize what is wrong in our lives. It corrects us when we are wrong and teaches us to do what is right. God uses it to prepare and equip His people to do every good work.

2 Timothy 3:16-17 NLT

Don't just listen to God's word. You must do what it says. Otherwise, you are only fooling yourselves. For if you listen to the word and don't obey, it is like glancing at your face in a mirror. You see yourself, walk away, and forget what you look like. But if you look carefully into the perfect law that sets you free, and if you do what it says and don't forget what you heard, then God will bless you for doing it.

James 1:22-25 NLT

69

You must understand that no prophecy of
Scripture came about by the prophet's own
interpretation of things. For prophecy never
had its origin in the human will, but prophets,
though human, spoke from God as they were
carried along by the Holy Spirit.

2 Peter 1:20-21 NIV

Jesus answered, "It is written: 'Man shall not
live on bread alone, but on every word that
comes from the mouth of God.'"

Matthew 4:4 NIV

We proclaim to you the One who existed from
the beginning ... He is the Word of life.

1 John 1:1 NLT

Whatever was written in former days
was written for our instruction, that through
endurance and through the encouragement
of the Scriptures we might have hope.

Romans 15:4 ESV

"Heaven and earth will pass away, but My
words will never pass away."

Matthew 24:35 NIV

For the word of God is alive and active.
Sharper than any double-edged sword, it
penetrates even to dividing soul and spirit,
joints and marrow; it judges the thoughts
and attitudes of the heart.

Hebrews 4:12 NIV

THE WORD OF GOD

The entirety of Your word is truth, and every one of Your righteous judgments endures forever.

Psalm 119:160 NKJV

Keep this Book of the Law always on your lips; meditate on it day and night, so that you may be careful to do everything written in it. Then you will be prosperous and successful.

Joshua 1:8 NIV

Blessed are those whose way is blameless, who walk in the law of the Lord! Blessed are those who keep His testimonies, who seek Him with their whole heart, who also do no wrong, but walk in His ways!

Psalm 119:1-3 ESV

"Blessed rather are those who hear the word of God and obey it."

Luke 11:28 NIV

"Everyone then who hears these words of Mine and does them will be like a wise man who built his house on the rock. And the rain fell, and the floods came, and the winds blew and beat on that house, but it did not fall, because it had been founded on the rock. And everyone who hears these words of Mine and does not do them will be like a foolish man who built his house on the sand. And the rain fell, and the floods came, and the winds blew and beat against that house, and it fell, and great was the fall of it."

Matthew 7:24-27 ESV

THE WORD OF GOD

Your word, LORD, is eternal; it stands firm in the heavens.

Psalm 119:89 NIV

The grass withers and the flowers fade beneath the breath of the LORD. And so it is with people. The grass withers and the flowers fade, but the word of our God stands forever.

Isaiah 40:7-8 NLT

I will worship toward Your holy temple, and praise Your name for Your lovingkindness and Your truth; for You have magnified Your word above all Your name.

Psalm 138:2 NKJV

As the Scriptures say, "People are like grass; their beauty is like a flower in the field. The grass withers and the flower fades. But the word of the Lord remains forever." And that word is the Good News that was preached to you.

1 Peter 1:24-25 NLT

In the beginning was the Word, and the Word was with God, and the Word was God.

John 1:1 ESV

The Word became flesh and made His dwelling among us. We have seen His glory, the glory of the one and only Son, who came from the Father, full of grace and truth.

John 1:14 NIV

GOD IS OUR SHIELD AND PORTION

The LORD is my strength and shield. I trust Him with all my heart. He helps me, and my heart is filled with joy. I burst out in songs of thanksgiving. The LORD gives His people strength. He is a safe fortress for His anointed king.

Psalm 28:7-8 NLT

The LORD is my rock and my fortress and my deliverer, my God, my rock, in whom I take refuge, my shield, and the horn of my salvation, my stronghold.

Psalm 18:2 ESV

My flesh and my heart may fail, but God is the strength of my heart and my portion forever.

Psalm 73:26 NIV

GOD IS OUR SHIELD AND PORTION

Our soul waits for the LORD; He is our help and our shield.

Psalm 33:20 NKJV

Every word of God is flawless; He is a shield to those who take refuge in Him.

Proverbs 30:5 NIV

You, O LORD, are a shield around me; You are my glory, the One who holds my head high.

Psalm 3:3 NLT

My shield is with God, who saves the upright in heart.

Psalm 7:10 ESV

GOD IS OUR SHIELD AND PORTION

You have given me Your shield of victory; Your help has made me great.

2 Samuel 22:36 NLT

Through the LORD's mercies we are not consumed, because His compassions fail not. They are new every morning; great is Your faithfulness. "The LORD is my portion," says my soul, "Therefore I hope in Him!"

Lamentations 3:22-24 NKJV

As for God, His way is perfect; the word of the LORD is proven; He is a shield to all who trust in Him.

2 Samuel 22:31 NKJV

GOD IS OUR SHIELD AND PORTION

The LORD is my portion; I promise to keep Your words. I entreat Your favor with all my heart; be gracious to me according to Your promise.

Psalm 119:57-58 ESV

He grants a treasure of common sense to the honest. He is a shield to those who walk with integrity.

Proverbs 2:7 NLT

You have given me the shield of Your salvation, and Your right hand supported me, and Your gentleness made me great.

Psalm 18:35 ESV

GOD IS OUR SHIELD AND PORTION

Then the LORD will appear over them; His arrow will flash like lightning. The Sovereign LORD will sound the trumpet; He will march in the storms of the south, and the LORD Almighty will shield them. They will destroy and overcome with slingstones. They will drink and roar as with wine; they will be full like a bowl used for sprinkling the corners of the altar.

Zechariah 9:14-15 NIV

Let all who take refuge in You rejoice; let them sing joyful praises forever. Spread Your protection over them, that all who love Your name may be filled with joy. For You bless the godly, O LORD; You surround them with Your shield of love.

Psalm 5:11-12 NLT

GOD IS OUR SHIELD AND PORTION

Praise be to the God and Father of our Lord Jesus Christ! In His great mercy He has given us new birth into a living hope through the resurrection of Jesus Christ from the dead, and into an inheritance that can never perish, spoil or fade. This inheritance is kept in heaven for you, who through faith are shielded by God's power until the coming of the salvation that is ready to be revealed in the last time.

1 Peter 1:3-5 NIV

I cried out to You, O LORD: I said, "You are my refuge, my portion in the land of the living."

Psalm 142:5 NKJV

You are my refuge and my shield; I have put my hope in Your word.

Psalm 119:114 NIV

81

GOD IS OUR SHIELD AND PORTION

The LORD is my rock, my fortress and my deliverer; my God is my rock, in whom I take refuge, my shield and the horn of my salvation. He is my stronghold, my refuge and my savior.

2 Samuel 22:2-3 NIV

How blessed you are, O Israel! Who else is like you, a people saved by the LORD? He is your protecting shield and your triumphant sword! Your enemies will cringe before you, and you will stomp on their backs!

Deuteronomy 33:29 NLT

Praise be to the LORD my Rock, who trains my hands for war, my fingers for battle. He is my loving God and my fortress, my stronghold and my deliverer, my shield, in whom I take refuge.

Psalm 144:1-2 NIV

Yea, when this flesh
and *heart* shall fail,
and mortal life shall cease,
I shall possess, within the veil,
a life of *joy* and *peace*.

A LIFE OF JOY

This is the day that the LORD has made; let us rejoice and be glad in it.

Psalm 118:24 ESV

Those who sow with tears will reap with songs of joy. Those who go out weeping, carrying seed to sow, will return with songs of joy, carrying sheaves with them.

Psalm 126:5-6 NIV

The LORD is my strength and song, and He has become my salvation.

Psalm 118:14 NKJV

Give praise to the LORD, proclaim His name; make known among the nations what He has done. Sing to Him, sing praise to Him; tell of all His wonderful acts. Glory in His holy name; let the hearts of those who seek the LORD rejoice.

Psalm 105:1-3 NIV

"Rejoice because your names are written in heaven."

Luke 10:20 NKJV

"Be happy! Yes, leap for joy! For a great reward awaits you in heaven."

Luke 6:23 NLT

A LIFE OF JOY

In Him our hearts rejoice, for we trust in His holy name.

Psalm 33:21 NIV

The joy of the LORD is your strength.

Nehemiah 8:10 NKJV

When Your words came, I ate them; they were my joy and my heart's delight.

Jeremiah 15:16 NIV

You turned my wailing into dancing; You removed my sackcloth and clothed me with joy.

Psalm 30:11 NIV

A LIFE OF JOY

Those who look to Him for help will be radiant with joy; no shadow of shame will darken their faces.

Psalm 34:5 NLT

Because You are my help, I sing in the shadow of Your wings.

Psalm 63:7 NIV

Many people say, "Who will show us better times?" Let Your face smile on us, LORD. You have given me greater joy than those who have abundant harvests of grain and new wine.

Psalm 4:6-7 NLT

A LIFE OF JOY

The precepts of the LORD are right, giving joy to the heart. The commands of the LORD are radiant, giving light to the eyes. The fear of the LORD is pure, enduring forever. The decrees of the LORD are firm, and all of them are righteous.

Psalm 19:8-9 NIV

Honor and majesty are before Him; strength and gladness are in His place.

1 Chronicles 16:27 NKJV

The LORD has done great things for us, and we are filled with joy.

Psalm 126:3 NIV

Let all those who seek You rejoice and be glad
in You; and let those who love Your salvation
say continually, "Let God be magnified!"

Psalm 70:4 NKJV

His anger lasts only a moment, but His favor
lasts a lifetime; weeping may remain for
a night, but rejoicing comes in the morning.

Psalm 30:5 NIV

Light shines on the godly, and joy on those
whose hearts are right. May all who are godly
rejoice in the LORD and praise His holy name!

Psalm 97:11-12 NLT

A LIFE OF JOY

Shouts of joy and victory resound in the tents of the righteous: "The LORD's right hand has done mighty things!"

Psalm 118:15 NIV

You make known to me the path of life; in Your presence there is fullness of joy; at Your right hand are pleasures forevermore.

Psalm 16:11 ESV

Rejoice in the LORD and be glad, you righteous; sing, all you who are upright in heart!

Psalm 32:11 NIV

"I am leaving you with a gift – peace of mind and heart. And the peace I give is a gift the world cannot give. So don't be troubled or afraid."

John 14:27 NLT

"In Me you may have peace. In the world you will have tribulation; but be of good cheer, I have overcome the world."

John 16:33 NKJV

Jesus said, "Come to Me, all of you who are weary and carry heavy burdens, and I will give you rest."

Matthew 11:28 NLT

FINDING PEACE

The mind governed by the flesh is death,
but the mind governed by the Spirit is life
and peace.

Romans 8:6 NIV

When a man's ways please the Lord, He makes
even his enemies to be at peace with him.

Proverbs 16:7 NKJV

The Lord gives strength to His people;
the Lord blesses His people with peace.

Psalm 29:11 NIV

FINDING PEACE

The peace of God, which surpasses all
understanding, will guard your hearts and
your minds in Christ Jesus.

Philippians 4:7 NKJV

Great peace have those who love Your law,
and nothing can make them stumble.

Psalm 119:165 NIV

Let the peace of Christ rule in your hearts,
to which indeed you were called in one body.
And be thankful.

Colossians 3:15 ESV

You will keep in perfect peace those whose minds are steadfast, because they trust in You. Trust in the LORD forever, for the LORD, the LORD Himself, is the Rock eternal.

Isaiah 26:3-4 NIV

I will both lie down in peace, and sleep; for You alone, O LORD, make me dwell in safety.

Psalm 4:8 NKJV

"Glory to God in the highest heaven, and on earth peace to those on whom His favor rests."

Luke 2:14 NIV

"Blessed are the peacemakers, for they
shall be called sons of God."

Matthew 5:9 ESV

Submit to God and be at peace with Him; in
this way prosperity will come to you.

Job 22:21 NIV

Because of God's tender mercy, the morning
light from heaven is about to break upon us,
to give light to those who sit in darkness and
in the shadow of death, and to guide us to the
path of peace.

Luke 1:78-79 NLT

The work of righteousness will be peace, and the effect of righteousness, quietness and assurance forever.

Isaiah 32:17 NKJV

The meek will inherit the land and enjoy peace and prosperity.

Psalm 37:11 NIV

May the God of hope fill you with all joy and peace as you trust in Him, so that you may overflow with hope by the power of the Holy Spirit.

Romans 15:13 NIV

Those who are peacemakers will plant seeds of peace and reap a harvest of righteousness.

James 3:18 NLT

The God of peace be with you.

Romans 15:33 NIV

The kingdom of God is not a matter of eating and drinking but of righteousness and peace and joy in the Holy Spirit.

Romans 14:17 ESV

God is not a God of confusion but of peace.

1 Corinthians 14:33 ESV

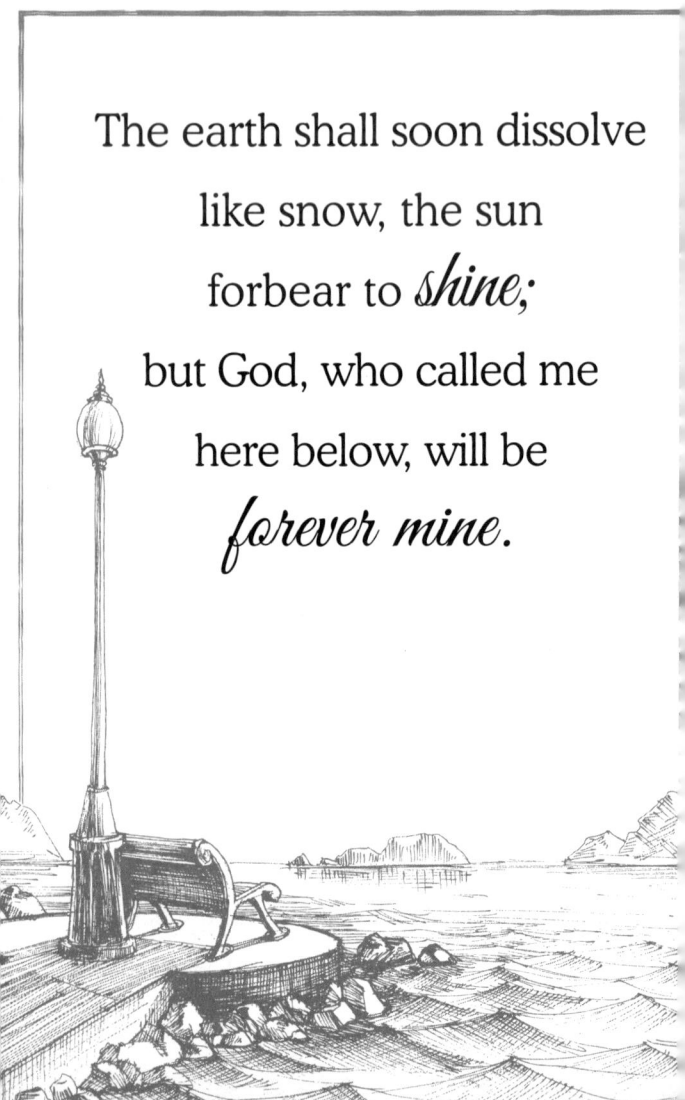

The earth shall soon dissolve like snow, the sun forbear to *shine;* but God, who called me here below, will be *forever mine.*

You are a chosen generation, a royal priesthood, a holy nation, His own special people, that you may proclaim the praises of Him who called you out of darkness into His marvelous light.

1 Peter 2:9 NKJV

He chose us in Him before the creation of the world to be holy and blameless in His sight. In love He predestined us for adoption to sonship through Jesus Christ, in accordance with His pleasure and will.

Ephesians 1:4-5 NIV

God is faithful, who has called you into fellowship with His Son, Jesus Christ our Lord.

1 Corinthians 1:9 NIV

In Him we were also chosen, having been predestined according to the plan of Him who works out everything in conformity with the purpose of His will, in order that we, who were the first to put our hope in Christ, might be for the praise of His glory.

Ephesians 1:11-12 NIV

God knew His people in advance, and He chose them to become like His Son, so that His Son would be the firstborn among many brothers and sisters. And having chosen them, He called them to come to Him. And having called them, He gave them right standing with Himself. And having given them right standing, He gave them His glory.

Romans 8:29-30 NLT

CALLED BY GOD

"You did not choose Me, but I chose you and appointed you that you should go and bear fruit and that your fruit should abide, so that whatever you ask the Father in My name, He may give it to you."

John 15:16 ESV

You are a holy people to the LORD your God; the LORD your God has chosen you to be a people for Himself, a special treasure above all the peoples on the face of the earth.

Deuteronomy 7:6 NKJV

You have been set apart as holy to the LORD your God, and He has chosen you from all the nations of the earth to be His own special treasure.

Deuteronomy 14:2 NLT

CALLED BY GOD

"Before I formed you in the womb I knew you, before you were born I set you apart; I appointed you as a prophet to the nations."

Jeremiah 1:5 NIV

He is Lord of lords and King of kings; and those who are with Him are called, chosen, and faithful.

Revelation 17:14 NKJV

To all who did receive Him, who believed in His name, He gave the right to become children of God, who were born, not of blood nor of the will of the flesh nor of the will of man, but of God.

John 1:12-13 ESV

CALLED BY GOD

Know that the LORD has set apart for Himself him who is godly; the LORD will hear when I call to Him.

Psalm 4:3 NKJV

Once you were not a people, but now you are God's people; once you had not received mercy, but now you have received mercy.

1 Peter 2:10 ESV

We are His workmanship, created in Christ Jesus for good works, which God prepared beforehand that we should walk in them.

Ephesians 2:10 NKJV

God chose you as firstfruits to be saved
through the sanctifying work of the Spirit
and through belief in the truth.

2 Thessalonians 2:13 NIV

"No one can come to Me unless the Father who
sent Me draws him. And I will raise him up on
the last day."

John 6:44 ESV

Let each person lead the life that the Lord has
assigned to him, and to which God has called
him.

1 Corinthians 7:17 ESV

CALLED BY GOD

Remember, dear brothers and sisters, that few of you were wise in the world's eyes or powerful or wealthy when God called you. Instead, God chose things the world considers foolish in order to shame those who think they are wise. And He chose things that are powerless to shame those who are powerful. God chose things despised by the world, things counted as nothing at all, and used them to bring to nothing what the world considers important.

1 Corinthians 1:26-28 NLT

He called you to salvation when we told you the Good News; now you can share in the glory of our Lord Jesus Christ.

2 Thessalonians 2:14 NLT

"Truly, truly, I say to you, whoever believes has eternal life."

John 6:47 ESV

"Everyone who lives in Me and believes in Me will never ever die."

John 11:26 NLT

Because Jesus lives forever, He has a permanent priesthood. Therefore He is able to save completely those who come to God through Him, because He always lives to intercede for them.

Hebrews 7:24-25 NIV

ETERNAL LIFE WITH THE LORD

"My Father's will is that everyone who looks to the Son and believes in Him shall have eternal life."

John 6:40 NIV

"God so loved the world that He gave His only begotten Son, that whoever believes in Him should not perish but have everlasting life."

John 3:16 NKJV

"Indeed, the time is coming when all the dead in their graves will hear the voice of God's Son, and they will rise again. Those who have done good will rise to experience eternal life, and those who have continued in evil will rise to experience judgment."

John 5:28-29 NLT

ETERNAL LIFE WITH THE LORD

Therefore we do not lose heart. Even though our outward man is perishing, yet the inward man is being renewed day by day. For our light affliction, which is but for a moment, is working for us a far more exceeding and eternal weight of glory.

2 Corinthians 4:16-17 NKJV

I write these things to you who believe in the name of the Son of God so that you may know that you have eternal life.

1 John 5:13 NIV

Whoever has the Son has life; whoever does not have the Son of God does not have life.

1 John 5:12 ESV

ETERNAL LIFE WITH THE LORD

He who believes in the Son has everlasting life; and he who does not believe the Son shall not see life, but the wrath of God abides on him.

John 3:36 NKJV

"You can enter God's Kingdom only through the narrow gate. The highway to hell is broad, and its gate is wide for the many who choose that way. But the gateway to life is very narrow and the road is difficult, and only a few ever find it."

Matthew 7:13-14 NLT

"Do not work for the food that perishes, but for the food that endures to eternal life, which the Son of Man will give to you. For on Him God the Father has set His seal."

John 6:27 ESV

Do not be deceived: God is not mocked, for whatever one sows, that will he also reap. For the one who sows to his own flesh will from the flesh reap corruption, but the one who sows to the Spirit will from the Spirit reap eternal life.

Galatians 6:7-8 ESV

"Father, the hour has come. Glorify Your Son, that Your Son may glorify You. For You granted Him authority over all people that He might give eternal life to all those You have given Him. Now this is eternal life: that they know You, the only true God, and Jesus Christ, whom You have sent."

John 17:1-3 NIV

ETERNAL LIFE WITH THE LORD

"Whoever drinks of this water will thirst again, but whoever drinks of the water that I shall give him will never thirst. But the water that I shall give him will become in him a fountain of water springing up into everlasting life."

John 4:13-14 NKJV

For the wages of sin is death, but the free gift of God is eternal life through Christ Jesus our Lord.

Romans 6:23 NLT

Where sin increased, grace increased all the more, so that, just as sin reigned in death, so also grace might reign through righteousness to bring eternal life through Jesus Christ our Lord.

Romans 5:20-21 NIV

ETERNAL LIFE WITH THE LORD

"I give them eternal life, and they shall never perish; no one will snatch them out of My hand. My Father, who has given them to Me, is greater than all; no one can snatch them out of My Father's hand. I and the Father are one."

John 10:28-30 NIV

"Teacher, what should I do to inherit eternal life?" Jesus replied, "What does the law of Moses say? How do you read it?" The man answered, "'You must love the Lord your God with all your heart, all your soul, all your strength, and all your mind.' And, 'Love your neighbor as yourself.'" "Right!" Jesus told him. "Do this and you will live!"

Luke 10:25-28 NLT

When we've been there
ten thousand years,
bright shining as the sun,
we've no less days to sing
God's praise
than when we'd
first begun.

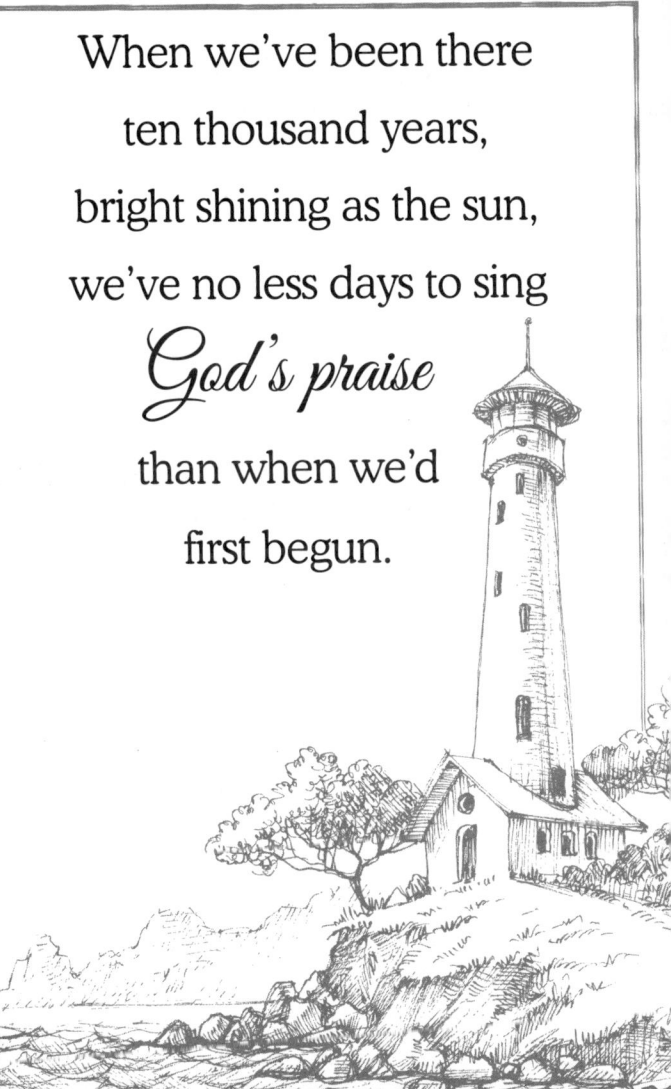

Sing praises to God and to His name! Sing loud praises to Him who rides the clouds. His name is the LORD – rejoice in His presence!

Psalm 68:4 NLT

Praise be to the LORD God, the God of Israel, who alone does marvelous deeds. Praise be to His glorious name forever; may the whole earth be filled with His glory.

Psalm 72:18-19 NIV

I will praise the LORD according to His righteousness, and will sing praise to the name of the LORD Most High.

Psalm 7:17 NKJV

PRAISE THE LORD

Let them praise the name of the LORD, for His name alone is exalted; His majesty is above earth and heaven.

Psalm 148:13 ESV

Praise the LORD! Sing to the LORD a new song. Sing His praises in the assembly of the faithful. O Israel, rejoice in your Maker. O people of Jerusalem, exult in your King.

Psalm 149:1-2 NLT

Declare His glory among the nations, His wonders among all peoples. For the LORD is great and greatly to be praised; He is also to be feared above all gods.

1 Chronicles 16:24-25 NKJV

PRAISE THE LORD

Let heaven and earth praise Him, the seas and all that move in them.

Psalm 69:34 NIV

LORD, You are my God. I will exalt You, I will praise Your name, for You have done wonderful things; Your counsels of old are faithfulness and truth.

Isaiah 25:1 NKJV

Praise Him, you highest heavens, and you waters above the heavens! Let them praise the name of the LORD! For He commanded and they were created. And He established them forever and ever; He gave a decree, and it shall not pass away.

Psalm 148:4-6 ESV

PRAISE THE LORD

Praise the LORD. Praise the LORD, you His servants; praise the name of the LORD. Let the name of the LORD be praised, both now and forevermore. From the rising of the sun to the place where it sets, the name of the LORD is to be praised.

Psalm 113:1-3 NIV

Praise the LORD, for the LORD is good;
sing praises to His name, for it is pleasant.

Psalm 135:3 NKJV

I will praise the name of God with a song;
I will magnify Him with thanksgiving.

Psalm 69:30 ESV

PRAISE THE LORD

Let everything that has breath praise the LORD. Praise the LORD.

Psalm 150:6 NIV

With all my heart I will praise You, O Lord my God. I will give glory to Your name forever, for Your love for me is very great.

Psalm 86:12-13 NLT

Praise the LORD, my soul; all my inmost being, praise His holy name. Praise the LORD, my soul, and forget not all His benefits – who forgives all your sins and heals all your diseases, who redeems your life from the pit and crowns you with love and compassion.

Psalm 103:1-4 NIV

PRAISE THE LORD

Sing praises to God, sing praises! Sing praises to our King, sing praises! For God is the King of all the earth; sing praises with a psalm!

Psalm 47:6-7 ESV

Let all that I am praise the LORD. O LORD my God, how great You are! You are robed with honor and majesty. You are dressed in a robe of light.

Psalm 104:1-2 NLT

Praise the LORD! I will praise the LORD with my whole heart, in the assembly of the upright and in the congregation. The works of the LORD are great, studied by all who have pleasure in them. His work is honorable and glorious, and His righteousness endures forever.

Psalm 111:1-3 NKJV

PRAISE THE LORD

Because Your steadfast love is better than life, my lips will praise You.

Psalm 63:3 ESV

Shout to the LORD, all the earth; break out in praise and sing for joy! Sing your praise to the LORD with the harp, with the harp and melodious song.

Psalm 98:4-5 NLT

I will exalt You, my God the King; I will praise Your name for ever and ever. Every day I will praise You and extol Your name for ever and ever.

Psalm 145:1-2 NIV

THANK THE LORD

Give thanks to the LORD and proclaim His greatness. Let the whole world know what He has done.

Psalm 105:1 NLT

Thanks be to God, who in Christ always leads us in triumphal procession, and through us spreads the fragrance of the knowledge of Him everywhere.

2 Corinthians 2:14 ESV

It is good to give thanks to the LORD, to sing praises to the Most High. It is good to proclaim Your unfailing love in the morning, Your faithfulness in the evening.

Psalm 92:1-2 NLT

Come, let us sing for joy to the LORD; let us shout aloud to the Rock of our salvation. Let us come before Him with thanksgiving and extol Him with music and song. For the LORD is the great God, the great King above all gods.

Psalm 95:1-3 NIV

You made all the delicate, inner parts of my body and knit me together in my mother's womb. Thank You for making me so wonderfully complex! Your workmanship is marvelous – how well I know it.

Psalm 139:13-14 NLT

Thanks be to God for His indescribable gift!

2 Corinthians 9:15 NKJV

THANK THE LORD

Enter His gates with thanksgiving and His courts with praise; give thanks to Him and praise His name. For the LORD is good and His love endures forever; His faithfulness continues through all generations.

Psalm 100:4-5 NIV

Thank God! He gives us victory over sin and death through our Lord Jesus Christ.

1 Corinthians 15:57 NLT

Oh give thanks to the LORD; call upon His name; make known His deeds among the peoples!

1 Chronicles 16:8 ESV

THANK THE LORD

We give thanks to You, O God, we give thanks! For Your wondrous works declare that Your name is near.

Psalm 75:1 NKJV

May you be filled with joy, always thanking the Father.

Colossians 1:11-12 NLT

Sing to the LORD with thanksgiving; sing praises on the harp to our God, who covers the heavens with clouds, who prepares rain for the earth, who makes grass to grow on the mountains.

Psalm 147:7-8 NKJV

THANK THE LORD

I will give thanks to the LORD with my whole heart; I will recount all of Your wonderful deeds. I will be glad and exult in You; I will sing praise to Your name, O Most High.

Psalm 9:1-2 ESV

Sing and make music from your heart to the Lord, always giving thanks to God the Father for everything, in the name of our Lord Jesus Christ.

Ephesians 5:19-20 NIV

Whatever you do, in word or deed, do everything in the name of the Lord Jesus, giving thanks to God the Father through Him.

Colossians 3:17 ESV

THANK THE LORD

Always be joyful. Never stop praying. Be thankful in all circumstances, for this is God's will for you who belong to Christ Jesus.

1 Thessalonians 5:16-18 NLT

The LORD is God, and He has made His light to shine upon us. You are my God, and I will give thanks to You; You are my God; I will extol You. Oh give thanks to the LORD, for He is good; for His steadfast love endures forever!

Psalm 118:27-29 ESV

Give thanks to the LORD! His mercy endures forever.

Psalm 106:1 NKJV

THANK THE LORD

"The one who offers thanksgiving as his sacrifice glorifies Me; to one who orders his way rightly I will show the salvation of God!"

Psalm 50:23 ESV

"Make thankfulness your sacrifice to God, and keep the vows you made to the Most High."

Psalm 50:14 NLT

Devote yourselves to prayer with an alert mind and a thankful heart.

Colossians 4:2 NLT

Give thanks to the LORD, for He is good; His love endures forever.

Psalm 107:1 NIV